French Parents Don't Give In

www.**transworldbooks**.co.uk

Also by Pamela Druckerman

Lust in Translation
French Children Don't Throw Food

For more information on Pamela Druckerman and her
books, see her website at www.pameladruckerman.com

French Parents Don't Give In

Pamela Druckerman

Doubleday

LONDON · TORONTO · SYDNEY · AUCKLAND · JOHANNESBURG

TRANSWORLD PUBLISHERS
61–63 Uxbridge Road, London W5 5SA
A Random House Group Company
www.transworldbooks.co.uk

First published in Great Britain
in 2013 by Doubleday
an imprint of Transworld Publishers

Published in the USA in 2013 as *Bébé Day by Day*

Illustrations by Margaux Motin

A CIP catalogue record for this book
is available from the British Library.

ISBN 9780857521637

Addresses for Random House Group Ltd companies outside the UK
can be found at: www.randomhouse.co.uk
The Random House Group Ltd Reg. No. 954009

The Random House Group Limited supports the Forest Stewardship Council (FSC®), the
leading international forest-certification organization. Our books carrying the FSC label are
printed on FSC®-certified paper. FSC is the only forest-certification scheme endorsed by
the leading environmental organizations, including Greenpeace. Our paper procurement
policy can be found at www.randomhouse.co.uk/environment

Typeset in Goudy 10.75/14pt by Falcon Oast Graphic Art Ltd
Printed and bound in Great Britain by
Clays Limited, Bungay, Suffolk

2 4 6 8 10 9 7 5 3 1

For Simon
and the individuals

Contents

Introduction

When I wrote a book about what I'd learned raising three kids in France, I wasn't sure that anyone besides my mother would read it. Actually, I wasn't even convinced that she would make it all the way through (she tends to prefer fiction).

But, to my surprise, many non-relatives read the book too. For a while there were lots of angry articles about it. Who was I to insult British and American parenting – if there really is such a thing? Surely there must be lots of little French brats? Had I only researched rich Parisians? Was I extolling socialism – or, worse, bottle-feeding?

I'm the sort of person who hears any criticism of herself and immediately thinks: that's so true! I fell into a funk. But then I started getting emails from ordinary parents like me. (I've posted many of these on my website.) I quickly cheered up. They didn't think I'd falsely accused Anglophones of having a parenting problem. Like me, they were living that problem, and they were eager to hear about an alternative.

Some parents told me that the book validated what they had already been doing privately – and often guiltily. Others said they'd tried the book's methods on their kids, and that these really did work. (No one was more relieved to hear this than me.) Many asked for more tips and specifics, or for a version of the book – without my personal back-story and voyage of discovery – that they could give as a kind of manual to grandparents, partners and babysitters.

This is that book. The 100 tips are my attempt to distil the smartest and most salient principles I've learned from French parents and childcare experts. You don't have to live in Paris to apply them. You don't even have to like cheese. (Though you should have a look at the recipes at the end of the book. They're a sampling of what kids in French nurseries eat, and they're delicious for grown-ups too.)

I believe in all 100 keys. But they're not my inventions, or my personal proclamations. And they're not all right for everyone. The French are very clear that every child is different, and that there are no recipes for raising kids. As you read the keys, you'll start to notice that behind many of the individual tips are a few guiding principles. One of these principles was radical for me, as an American: if family life is centred entirely on the children, it's not good for anyone, not even for the kids.

I think American parents have already worked this out. Statistics show that as this new intensive style of parenting has taken hold – the one that's popped up seemingly out of nowhere in the last twenty years – marital satisfaction has fallen. Parents are famously less happy than non-parents, and they become more unhappy with each additional child. (Working mothers in Texas apparently prefer housework to childcare.) The most depressing study of middle-class American families I've read describes how parents have gone from being authority figures to being 'valet[s] for the child'. Given

the amount of cooking-to-order and schlepping
around that goes on, I would add 'personal chefs' and
'chauffeurs' too.

The clincher is that we're starting to doubt whether
this demanding style of parenting is even good for
children. Many of our good intentions – from baby-
brain-training videos to the all-consuming quest for the
best university place – now seem to be of questionable
value. Some experts call the first generation of kids to
graduate from this brand of child-rearing 'teacups'
because they're so fragile, and warn that the way we're
defining success is making these children quite unhappy.

Obviously, French parents don't do everything right.
And they don't all do the same things. The tips in this
book refer to conventional wisdom. They are what
French parenting books, magazines and experts generally
say you should do – and what most of the middle-class
parents I know actually do do, or at least believe they
should be doing. (Though a French friend of mine said
she planned to give a copy to her brother, so he could
'become more French'.)

A lot of 'French' wisdom just feels like common
sense. I've received letters from readers describing the
overlaps between French parenting and Montessori, or
the teachings of a Hungarian-born woman called Magda
Gerber. Others assure me that we Americans used to
bring up our kids this way too, before Reaganomics, the
psychotherapy boom and that study which said that poor

children don't hear enough words when they're little. (Let's just say that the American middle class massively overcompensated.)

But some French ideas have a power and elegance that's all their own. French parents widely believe that babies are rational, that you should combine a little bit of strictness with a lot of freedom, and that you should listen carefully to children, but not feel obliged to do everything they say. Their ability to move their offspring on from 'children's foods' is remarkable. Above all, the French think that the best parenting happens when you're calm. What's really neat is that, in France, you have an entire nation, in real time, trying to follow these principles. It's like a country-sized control group. Come and visit. You'll be amazed.

French parenting is particularly relevant to us now because it's a kind of mirror image of what's been happening in Britain and America. We Anglophones tend to think you should teach children cognitive skills such as reading as soon as possible; the French focus instead on 'soft' skills like socializing and empathy in the early years. We want our kids to be stimulated a lot; they think down-time is just as crucial. We often hesitate to frustrate a child; they think a child who can't cope with frustration will grow up miserable. We're focused on the outcomes of parenting; they think the quality of the eighteen or so years you'll spend living together counts for a lot too. We tend to think that long-term sleep deprivation, routine *tantrums, picky eating and constant interruptions are more or less inevitable when you have small children. They believe these things are – please imagine me saying this in a French accent – impossible.*

I'm a journalist, not a parenting expert. So what really sold me on French principles was the data. Many things that French parents do by intuition, tradition or trial-and-error are exactly what the latest English-language research recommends. The French take for granted that you can teach little babies how to sleep through the night; that patience can be learned; that too much praise can be damaging for children; that you should become attuned to a baby's rhythms; that toddlers don't need flash cards; and that tasting foods makes you like those foods. Science is now telling us this too. (To keep the tips simple, I've listed many of the relevant studies in the bibliography on page 177.)

Please take this book as inspiration, not doctrine. And be flexible. One of the French sayings I didn't have room for was 'You have to keep changing what you do.' Kids evolve quickly. As they do, you can keep the same guiding principles, but you may need to apply them differently. I hope that this book helps make that possible. Rather than giving lots of specific rules, it's more like a toolbox to help parents work things out on their own. As the old saying goes: don't give a man a filet de saumon à la vapeur de fenouil. *Just teach him how to fish.*

Pregnancy

A Croissant in
the Oven

All pregnant women worry. You're making a human being, after all. Some of us can barely make dinner. But in Britain and America, worrying is practically an Olympic sport. We feel we must choose a parenting philosophy, and weigh up whether each bite of food we eat is in the baby's best interest. All this angst doesn't feel pleasant. But to many of us, it does feel necessary. We're signalling that there's nothing we won't sacrifice for our unborn child.

The French don't encourage this anxiety. Instead, in the word cloud of French pregnancy, terms like 'serenity', 'balance' and 'zen' keep popping up. Mothers-to-be are expected to signal their competence by showing how calm they are, and by demonstrating that they still experience pleasure. This small shift in emphasis makes a very big difference.

1.

Pregnancy is not a research project

French mothers-to-be might read a baby book or two, but they don't baby-proof their homes beyond recognition, or select a stroller as if they were choosing a husband. There is an important difference between being prepared and being the person who recites the names of chromosomal disorders at dinner.

Making a baby is more mysterious and meaningful than anything you've ever done (unless you've been pregnant before, or had cats). You can dwell on the enormity of that without trying to micromanage your pregnancy, and without anointing a personal guru. The most important voice to have inside your head is your own.

2.

Calm is better for Bébé

If you're not persuaded to be calm for your own sake, do it for your unborn child. French pregnancy magazines say that the foetus senses his mother's moods. He's jolted by too much stress, and soothed when pleasure hormones cross the placenta. Experts urge pregnant women to discuss their concerns with a doctor or therapist and to pamper themselves with pedicures, romantic nights out (preferably with the baby's father) and lunches with friends. According to the French, the resulting *zen maman* pops out a *bébé zen*, and a calm pregnancy sets the tone for calm parenting.

3.

French mothers eat sushi (sometimes)

France's future *mamans* try to keep the risks in perspective. They know that some things – like cigarettes and alcohol – are categorically hazardous for the unborn child. French doctors now advise going cold turkey on both (though some pregnant women still have the occasional *coupe de champagne*). But other things are dangerous only if they happen to be contaminated. Sushi, salami, uncooked shellfish, raw eggs and unpasteurized cheese are in this category. This is not to say that you should rush out and eat oysters. Listen to the advice of your doctor or midwife. Just remember that accidentally eating unpasteurized Parmesan cheese with your pasta is not grounds for a nervous breakdown.

4.

The baby doesn't need brioche

In France, pregnancy isn't an excuse to devour the foods you've been denying yourself – or guiltily bingeing on – since adolescence. If your body cries out for doughnuts, distract it by eating an apple or a piece of cheese. French women's long-term strategy is to enjoy the occasional bowl of *mousse au chocolat*. This quells the beast, and makes it less likely that they'll go overboard on sweet foods later. This practice of moderation, not self-deprivation, could explain why a recent French pregnancy book is called *Emergency: She Wants Strawberries*.

5.

Eat for one (and a bit)

Do like the French, and plan to emerge from pregnancy with your figure and your feminine allure intact. Remember that it will be much easier to lose the baby-weight if you haven't put on too much while pregnant. Take your doctor's weight-gain limits seriously. The French limits are lower than British and American ones, and women treat them like holy edicts. One French guide says that a moderately active pregnant woman needs an additional 200 to 500 calories per day, but warns that anything more 'inevitably turns into fat'. This careful eating needn't feel austere. Crucially, French women don't eat merely to nourish the foetus. They also aim to eat for pleasure.

6.

Don't borrow your husband's shirts

Dressing like a shapeless blob is bad for morale (yours and your mate's, possibly even the baby's). Take a tip from Parisiennes, and don't lose your sense of style just because you're pregnant. Invest strategically in a few flattering maternity clothes. Then convert cardigans and leggings from your wardrobe into pregnancy gear, and brighten yourself up with lipstick and coloured scarves. Attention to these details signals that you're not graduating from 'woman' to 'mum'. You can be both.

7.

Don't lose your mojo

French pregnancy magazines don't just say that it's OK
to have sex; they spell out exactly how to do it –
including lists of pregnancy-safe sex toys (nothing with
batteries), aphrodisiacs (mustard, cinnamon, chocolate)
and detailed instructions on how to manoeuvre yourself
into third-trimester positions. Accompanying fashion
spreads show pregnant women in lacy maternity lingerie
with come-hither looks. Pregnant French women don't
morph into sex goddesses; they have the same fluctuating
libidos as the rest of us. But they don't behave as if
they've crossed into a realm where intimacy is on hold.
They know that if you put your seductive powers in the
deep freeze, it's hard to thaw them out later.

8.

Epidurals aren't evil

The French don't view childbirth as a heroic test of pain tolerance, or as early evidence of the trials a mother will be willing to undergo for her child. French women don't typically launch their babies into the world amid a frenzy of micromanagement in which they specify the lighting, the guest list, and who gets to catch the baby when it comes out.

There are midwives, pre-natal baby whisperers and even some home births in France. The French don't think there's anything wrong with giving birth the way you want to. But they believe the main aim is to get the baby safely from your uterus into your arms. While some things may be better *au naturel* (breasts and maple syrup come to mind), others are better with a giant dose of drugs. Even French women who subsist on organic food and plan to breastfeed well into pre-school are delighted when the anaesthetist arrives.

9.

Papa: don't stand at the business end

Unless you are actually delivering the baby, don't stand at the 'end of the tunnel' during the final moments of labour. Yes, there's the miracle of life to witness. Of course you want to seem welcoming to your child. But consider meeting him half a second later, in order to preserve your partner's feminine mystique. It gets messy down there. As the French saying goes, not all truths should be told.

Babyhood

Bébé Einstein

The French believe that babies aren't helpless blobs. They treat even newborns like tiny, rational people who understand language and can learn things (when they're taught gently, and at their own pace). This isn't quite as far-fetched as it sounds. American scientists have recently proved that babies aren't blank slates: they can make moral judgements, assess probabilities and do basic maths. Who knows what baby superpowers they will discover next? At the very least, we should remember that when we talk, babies might be listening.

10.

Give your baby a tour de la maison

Like anyone entering their new home for the first time,
your baby wants to get oriented, and to know where
she'll be sleeping. When you bring her back from the
hospital (or emerge from the bathtub after that awesome
home birth), show her around. This is it: home base!
'Here is Mummy and Daddy's room, and here is your
room.' Some French parents make a practice of saying
goodbye to their baby when they're going out and telling
her when they'll be back. They help her make sense of
the world by explaining that Grandma is Daddy's (or
Mummy's) mother, and what that new sound is outside.
The French believe that when they speak to a baby,
they're not just comforting her with the sound of their
voice; they're conveying important information. They
think that treating a baby like a rational person helps to
reassure her, and – if she's upset – to calm her down.

11.

Observe your baby

When you ask a French new mother what her parenting philosophy is, she'll often shrug and say, 'I just observe my baby.' She means that she spends a lot of time watching what her baby does. This is more important – and less obvious – than it sounds. She's trying to tune in to her baby's experience, and learn to read and follow her baby's cues. (American scientists call this 'sensitivity' and say it's one of the most important qualities in a care-giver.) You want to be there when your baby needs you. But when she's happily babbling and drooling on her play mat, try to just let her be. You are striving to achieve what the French call '*complicité*' – complicity – mutual trust and understanding, even with someone who regularly throws up on you.

12.

Tell your baby the truth

France's most famous parenting expert, Françoise Dolto, said that children don't need family life to be perfect. But they do need it to be coherent, and not secret. She said that babies can sense when there's a problem in the home, and need the same comforting confirmation we all do: 'You're not nuts! Something really is wrong!' From when a baby is six months old, parents should tell her if they're getting divorced. When a grandparent dies, parents should gently explain this, and briefly bring the child to the funeral. An adopted child needs to hear about her birth mother, even if the adoptive mother simply says, 'I don't know her, but you knew her.' From the earliest stage, the French believe that sensitively telling children the truth is the best way to make them feel safe.

13.

Be polite to your baby

French parents tend not to speak down to their infants in sing-song baby talk. However, they do pay them the courtesy of saying '*bonjour*', 'please' and 'thank you'. If you believe that your baby understands you, then it's never too early to start modelling good manners. And this early *politesse* sets the tone for calm and respectful relations later.

14.

French parents don't over-stimulate

Like the rest of us, the French believe that you should talk to your baby, show her things and read her books. But they don't think a mother should spend eight hours a day talking non-stop to her infant like an irritating house guest. Babies need down-time. They don't want to be constantly watched and spoken to.

Let interactions and conversations follow a natural rhythm. Give your baby a chance to roll around in a safe space and be free. When parents allow this, they're not being neglectful or missing key synapse-building moments. *Au contraire*, babies need time to assimilate all the new information they've been taking in. Their parents need some time off too.

15.

Nudge your baby on to a schedule

For the first few months, French parents usually feed babies on demand. After that, they take a few things for granted:

- The baby should eat at more or less the same times each day.
- A few big feeds are better than lots of small ones.
- Babies can adjust to the family's normal eating rhythm.

With these ideas in mind, you can gradually stretch out the amount of time between feeds. Distract your baby from pangs of hunger by taking her for a walk, or strapping her into a carrier. At first, you might only gain a few extra minutes a day between feeds. But your baby will get used to waiting a bit. Eventually she'll get to three hours between feeds, and before long to four. Soon she'll be on roughly the same eating pattern she'll be likely to follow for the rest of her childhood: breakfast, lunch and dinner, plus an afternoon snack. (This roughly corresponds to 8 am, noon, 4 pm and 8 pm, but nobody in France expects this schedule to be observed with military precision.)

16.

Baby formula isn't poison

French mothers know that breast is best, but they don't
treat breastfeeding as a measure of the mum. Many
point out that they themselves are healthy, despite
having drunk a lot of powdered formula as infants – back
when it was the old, inferior version. (Other factors
contribute to their good health, but still.) Although
some breastfeeding guilt is encroaching in France, in
general, mothers think it's unhealthy and unpleasant to
breastfeed under moral duress, or to keep nursing
through Dantesque trials of pain and inconvenience.
They believe that whether and how long to nurse should
be your personal decision, not one for the mothers in
your NCT group. The best reason to breastfeed, they say,
is if you and your baby enjoy it.

17.

Vegetables are a French child's first food

If your baby's first food is bland rice cereal, she'll probably take to it. But why not start with something more exciting? French parents usually feed their babies flavour-packed puréed spinach, carrots, courgettes and other vegetables from about the age of six months. They soon move on to fruits, small portions of meat and different types of fish. By introducing lots of different foods at an early age, they are trying to launch their children on a lifelong relationship with these flavours and introduce them to the pleasures of eating.

Sleep

Rock-a-bye Bébé

Here's a paradox: French babies often sleep through the night by the age of three or four months, or even sooner. Yet their parents don't make them 'cry it out' for hours on end.

This isn't a coincidence, a mystery, or the result of adding cognac to their milk. It's simply what is expected. If you believe that little babies can learn things, then it follows that you can teach them things. And one of the things you can often teach them, early on, is how to sleep.

18.

Understand the science of sleep

Your baby is unique and adorable. There will one day undoubtedly be a biopic about his life, in which an ageing Gwyneth Paltrow plays you, as his elderly but still ravishing mother. However, as French parents know, even your own baby is subject to the laws of science. And one of these laws is that all healthy babies, even yours, sleep in brief cycles. At the end of each cycle, they usually wake up and cry a bit.

The key to your baby sleeping for longer stretches is for him to learn how to connect his sleep cycles on his own. He needs to be able to plunge from one sleep cycle straight into the next one, without anyone else having to get out of bed. Grown-ups – except for the insomniacs among us – manage this same feat every night. Connecting sleep cycles is a skill. A few lucky babies are born with it. Most have to practise before they master it.

19.

Babies are noisy sleepers

Infants make a lot of noise when they sleep. They whine. They wave their arms around like traffic cops. This does not mean they are awake. If you race into their rooms or pick them up the instant they make a peep, you will sometimes wake them up.

20.

Practise 'la Pause'

We know that babies often cry when they're learning to connect their sleep cycles. We also know that they can make a noise like an angry frog and yet still be asleep. So once the baby is a few weeks old, don't instantly jump up when he cries at night. Do like the French, and pause for a few minutes.

You are waiting to see if, this time, your baby will have a breakthrough moment and plunge into the next sleep cycle on his own, without anyone else's help. If you immediately rush in and pick him up, he won't have a chance to develop this skill.

Maybe he isn't ready to connect his cycles yet. But if you don't pause, you won't know, and neither will he. He'll think he needs you to put him back to sleep at the end of each cycle. Rushing in to him may make you feel like a devoted parent, but in effect you're treating your baby like a helpless blob who is not ready to learn and grow.

You needn't pause for very long. Some French parents wait five minutes, others wait a bit more or less. They're not letting their baby 'cry it out'. If he's still crying after these few minutes, then they reason that he must need something, and they pick him up. (As you get to know your baby's cries better, you may well come to recognize his get-me-out-of-this-wet-nappy cry. When you hear that one, you don't need to pause – just change him.)

21.

Set the mood for sleep

The Pause is not enough in itself to teach babies how to sleep. The French believe that you should also have rituals that set the right tone for bedtime. Keep your baby in daylight during the day, even when he's napping. Signal to him that the big night-time sleep is approaching by giving him a bath, changing him into pyjamas, singing a lullaby and saying goodnight. Once he's calm and relaxed, but preferably still awake, put him to bed in a dark room. Spending cosy time together before bed matters. You want to send your baby off to sleep feeling secure enough to know that he can separate from you for a little while and still be OK.

22.

Try the talking cure

Why talk to everyone else about how your baby sleeps
except the baby himself? Tell him it's bedtime. Explain
that the whole family needs rest. Say that you're going
to wait a few minutes before you come in to him,
because you want him to be able to fall asleep again on
his own. Tell him how nice it will be for everyone –
including him – when he no longer needs to wake up at
3 am. One French baby book says that after a baby
sleeps through the night for the first time, his parents
should congratulate him and tell him how pleased and
proud they are. Doing this will help lock in the baby's
new-found ability.

23.

Sleeping well is better for the baby

French parents don't teach their babies to sleep soundly just for their own convenience. They believe that sleeping well is in the child's best interest too. Research backs them up: a baby who sleeps poorly can become hyperactive and irritable – among many other troubles. (My personal studies suggest that the same is true for sleep-deprived mothers.)

Sleep also contains an important symbolic lesson for babies: learning to sleep well is part of learning to be part of the family. Babies eventually need to adapt to what others around them need too. Three months – the age by which many French babies sleep through the night – is the point when French maternity leave usually ends and many *mamans* need to be fresh for work in the morning.

24.

Trust that your baby will 'do his nights'

Don't expect any of this to work immediately. It probably won't. But stick with it and remain confident that your baby will, as the French say, 'do his nights'. Convey this confidence to your baby (doing so really helps). Believe that if you keep gently and patiently teaching your baby how to sleep well, he will eventually learn – often just when your own sleep-deprivation experiment starts to feel unbearable.

25.

If you miss the window for the Pause, let your baby cry it out

The gentle sleep-teaching method of the Pause works best in a baby's first four months. When parents miss this window, French experts often suggest doing some form of 'controlled crying' – leaving the baby to cry for a longer period. You can talk to the baby about this too. It generally succeeds within a few nights.

Food

Bébé Gourmet

Imagine a planet where family mealtimes are pleasant, children eat the same foods as their parents and few children get fat. That planet is France. But none of this happens automatically. French parents set out to teach their children how to eat well, and they work at it assiduously. Their efforts pay off four times a day. The moral of the French food story is: treat your child like a budding foodie and she will (gradually) rise to the occasion.

26.

There are no 'children's' foods

You can find chicken nuggets, fish fingers and pizza in France. But these are occasional treats for kids, not daily fare. French parents almost never let their kids become picky eaters who survive on mono-diets of pasta and white rice. Starting from a very young age, children mostly eat the same foods as their parents. The weekly menu at Paris's state-run nurseries consists of four-course meals (including a cheese course) that resemble something you would order in a bistro. (See some favourite crèche recipes, and a weekly crèche menu, on page 153.)

27.

There's just one snack a day

I used to find it hard to imagine kids going from breakfast to lunch without as much as a raisin in between. But it turns out that this is possible, and even pleasant. Typically, French children eat only at mealtimes and at the afternoon snack, called the *goûter*.

If a child doesn't snack between meals, she'll actually be hungry by mealtimes, so she will eat more. And there's something calming about not regarding every moment as a potential eating opportunity. You can all get on with other things. Once you're in the swing of this one-snack system, the *goûter* becomes a special occasion every day. It's usually a combination of sweets and fruit. Often there's some chocolate. One classic *goûter* is a piece of dark chocolate in a piece of baguette – a chocolate sandwich – with a mini-carton of fruit juice.

28.

Don't solve a crisis with a cookie

Not producing a biscuit whenever your child whines can have far-reaching benefits. First, you're not rewarding her outburst, so you're not encouraging her to whine again. Second, you're teaching her not to eat just because she's upset. She'll thank you when she's thirty and can still fit into her high-school jeans.

29.

You are the keeper of the fridge

French children generally don't have the right to open the refrigerator and help themselves to whatever they want. They have to ask their parents first. This doesn't just cut down on the snacking in the house. It also cuts down on the chaos.

30.

Make your child your sous-chef

The five-year-old French girl who lives next door to us measures and mixes the oil, vinegar, mustard and salt for the family's vinaigrette all by herself, while her mum is cooking the main course. It's no coincidence that this little girl loves salad. We all feel more involved with foods that we've had a hand in preparing. (Just think how much you want everyone to eat the dinner you've just made.)

I've seen French two-year-olds sit at the kitchen counter tearing up spinach. Three-year-olds learn to peel cucumbers, cut tomatoes and mix the batter for crêpes. Parents oversee this process and don't mind a little mess. Plus, they know there's no better time to find out about their child's day at nursery school than when they are peeling the shells off hard-boiled eggs together.

When the cooking is done, eat as the French typically do: together, at the table, with the television off.

31.

Serve food in courses, vegetables first

Your family meals don't need to be fancy. You don't need to light candles or drape a white napkin over your arm. Just bring out some vegetables before anything else. If your kids haven't been snacking all day, they will be hungry and more likely to eat what's put in front of them first. (The same strategy works at breakfast with cut-up fruit.) A vegetable starter doesn't have to be elaborate. It can be a bowl of sugar-snap peas, some cut-up cherry tomatoes with a dash of olive oil and balsamic vinegar, or some sautéed broccoli. Just put a serving on each child's plate and wait. Then follow with a main course, and dessert.

32.

Everyone eats the same thing

In France, children don't decide what they'll have for dinner. There are no choices or customizations. There's just one meal – the same one for everyone.

It's safe to try this at home. If your child refuses to eat something, react neutrally. Don't offer her something else instead. If you're just emerging from a kids' food ghetto, start by making family meals that you know she likes, then gradually introduce more adventurous new dishes.

Above all, stay positive and calm. Give the new rules time to settle. Remember that you're crediting your child with being grown-up enough to eat the same foods as you. Accompany the new rules with some new freedoms, like letting her cut the quiche, or sprinkle the Parmesan cheese herself. Let her choose what kind of fruit to have for dessert, or whether to put jam or honey in her yogurt. When you eat in a restaurant, let her order what she wants, within reason.

33.

You just have to taste it

Most kids like ice cream from the first taste (though mine complained that it was 'too cold'). However, many foods take some warming up to. The fact that they're new puts kids off, and it's only through trying these foods over and over again that they start to like them.

This is the cornerstone of the way the French feed their children. Kids are expected to take at least one bite of every dish on the table. I'm sure there are French families who don't consider this rule to be sacred and infallible, but I have yet to meet them.

Present the tasting rule to your child as if it's a law of nature – like gravity. Explain that our tastes are shaped by what we eat. If she's nervous about trying something for the first time, let her just pick up a piece and sniff it (often a little nibble will follow). One new food per meal is enough. Serve it alongside something you know she likes.

Oversee this process without acting like a prison guard. Be calm and even playful about it. After she takes the requisite bite, acknowledge this. React neutrally if she says she doesn't like it. Never offer a replacement food. Remember, you're playing the long game. You don't want her to eat an artichoke once, under duress. You want her to gradually learn to like artichokes.

34.

Keep broccoli in the mix

Even if a certain food isn't a hit, make sure it keeps making regular appearances at dinner. Put broccoli in soup, sprinkle some cheese on it, or stir-fry it. Broccoli might never be your daughter's favourite food, but with each taste it will get closer to being part of her repertoire. She'll come to regard it as normal. Once it's solidly established, make sure it turns up at least every few weeks. Ultimately, your child won't love all foods. But she'll give each one a chance.

35.

You choose the foods, she chooses how much

Your child knows (or should learn to know) when she's had enough. Serve smallish portions, and don't pressurize her to clear her plate. Wait and see if she asks for seconds before serving more. If she asks for a third helping of pasta, offer her a yogurt or some cheese instead.

Remember that the goal isn't to cajole enough nutrients into her mouth at every sitting; it's to guide her into becoming an independent eater who enjoys a variety of foods and regulates her own appetite. If she doesn't eat enough at one meal, she'll catch up at the next one. If she's always snacking, she'll never learn to eat at mealtimes.

36.

Variety, variety

The French are nuts about variety. They serve their children lots of different foods, prepared lots of different ways. They aim for a variety of textures and colours, too. This has many benefits:

- Kids get a variety of nutrients. They're more likely to eat a balanced diet if they eat a variety of foods.
- It makes mealtimes more peaceful. If your child is used to different foods, she won't erupt at the sight of a piece of parsley in her soup.
- It's more social. You can take your child anywhere and she'll find something she likes. You won't have to keep apologizing to hosts who don't serve plain pasta. You build complicity with your child as you roll with it together.
- It's more pleasurable for the child. Her world will expand as she discovers different smells, textures and tastes.
- It shows your confidence in her. If you treat your child like a food adventurer, she'll eventually live up to your expectations. Whereas if you treat her

like a finicky eater who can only handle grilled cheese and the occasional banana, that's what she'll become.

37.

French kids drink water

In France, tap water is the de facto drink for the family at lunch and dinner, and any time in between. Parents don't take drink orders, they just put a jug of water on the table. (This quickly becomes a habit.) Juice is for breakfast, and for the occasional afternoon snack. Sugary fizzy drinks are for special occasions like parties. Period. *Santé*!

38.

Looks matter

Everyone is more drawn to food that looks appetizing. In Parisian restaurants, almost as much thought goes into presenting food as cooking it. That can be your principle at home, too. Put take-away on to serving plates. Garnish a monotone dinner with cherry tomatoes or some grated carrots. Enlist your kids to artfully arrange raw vegetables by colour on a platter, or set out plates of raw ingredients that they can use to assemble colourful sandwich melts, which you then grill for them. From the age of two or three, French children often use grown-up plates and glasses like their parents, rather than plastic ones. This signals that they're equal eaters, and it makes the whole table look better.

39.

Talk about food

French people talk a lot about food. That's partly how they convey to their children that eating isn't just about nutrition – it's a full-on pleasure. Experts suggest getting beyond 'I like it / I don't like it' by asking your child questions such as: do you think this apple is sour or sweet? How does mackerel taste different from salmon? I prefer red-leaf lettuce to rocket – what do you think?

Treat food as a conversation-starter. When the cake collapses or the stew burns, laugh about it together. At the supermarket, take a walking tour of the greengrocer's section and let your child choose some fruits and vegetables. (One of my sons likes to ride in the shopping trolley wielding a giant leek.)

Above all, keep the food chat positive. If your child abruptly announces that she doesn't like pears any more, calmly ask what she's decided to like instead.

40.

Keep the day's nutritional balance in mind

French parents tend to carry around a little mental map of what their children eat each day. They expect them to get most of their protein at lunchtime, whereas dinner will centre on grains and vegetables. They typically keep sweet foods for lunchtime dessert and *goûter*. Dinner-time dessert is usually yogurt or cheese, and fruit. ('What you eat in the evening just stays with you for years,' one French mother explained to me.)

41.

Dinner shouldn't involve hand-to-hand combat

A French nutritionist says her best advice is not to let your child see how desperately you want her to eat her vegetables. Don't puff up with exaggerated food cheer either. Play it cool. Those *haricots verts* you've just placed on the table are not the second coming. The tone you're aiming for at mealtimes is cheerful nonchalance. Just be calmly positive about food. Tell kids that meals are a time for the whole family to be together and to enjoy each other's company.

42.

Eat chocolate

The French don't treat sweets like Kryptonite, or try to
convince their children that refined sugar doesn't exist.
That would just make them more likely to go overboard
when they finally got their hands on some. Instead, they
teach their kids that sweets are occasional treats to enjoy
in controlled doses. French children eat small helpings
of chocolate or cookies on a regular basis. They'll often
have cake for the afternoon *goûter* at weekends – just
not too much. On special occasions such as parties,
parents tend to give their children free rein. We all need
some time away from the regular rules.

43.

Keep meals short and sweet

Dinner is not a hostage situation. Don't expect young children to stay at the table for more than twenty or thirty minutes. Teach them to ask to be liberated. But when they do, let them go. Mealtimes will get longer as kids get older.

In restaurants, leaving the table usually isn't an option. Plan these outings carefully. Make sure that children arrive hungry, and not exhausted. Bring some books or drawing supplies. Before you go inside, explain even to little children that special rules apply – one of which is that they can choose what they'll eat. Remind them to be '*sage*' – calm and in command of themselves. (Unlike the English equivalent 'be good', *sage* suggests a certain wisdom and capacity for self-control.)

Learning
Sooner Isn't Better

It is tempting to think of early childhood as the start of a marathon, and the finishing line as admission to university (winners go to Oxbridge). In this analogy you'd want to get your kids off to a fast start – talking, reading and doing maths as early as possible. You might buy them flashcards, brain-training toys, or a special contraption to help them learn to walk.

The French want their children to be successful too. (They have their own version of Oxbridge called the 'grandes écoles'.) But they probably wouldn't use the marathon analogy. They don't tend to think there's any point rushing young children through developmental milestones, or teaching them skills like reading and maths before they are optimally ready for them. French pre-schoolers do learn some letters, but they don't actually learn to read until about the age of six. (Finnish teenagers have the highest average reading and maths scores in the Western world, and kids there don't learn to read until they're seven.)

The latest research validates this slower approach. It turns out that it's more important to teach pre-schoolers skills like concentration, getting along with others and self-control (more about self-control in the next chapter). These abilities create a stronger basis for later academic success than maths worksheets or pre-literacy training. And as the French can affirm, avoiding the baby marathon is a lot more pleasant for both parents and kids.

44.

Don't teach your toddler how to read

Yes, it's technically possible to teach a three-year-old how to recognize words. But what's the rush? You don't want to take time away from reading to your child and teaching him the things he most needs to learn at this age, like how to be organized, articulate and empathetic. French nursery schools encourage children to have conversations, finish projects and tackle problems. In my daughter's Parisian reception class one day, the assignment was for twenty-five illiterate five-year-olds to give talks on 'justice' or 'courage'. When these kids are six, they'll learn to read far more quickly than they would have done at three.

45.

Let your child set the pace

The French have a saying: 'You can't go faster than the music'. They believe that a child will roll over, rise to his feet, become potty trained and start to talk when he's good and ready. Lovingly encourage and support him – don't try to rush his development or turn his childhood into boot camp. Being a little kid shouldn't be hard work. There's time enough for that later.

46.

Teach the four magic words

Our magic words are 'please' and 'thank you'. The French have those, plus two more: 'hello' and 'goodbye'. They're especially zealous about making their children say '*bonjour*' as soon as they walk into somebody's house. Children don't get to slouch in under the cover of their parents' greeting.

French parents view *bonjour* not only as a matter of politeness, but also a critical lesson in empathy. Saying it forces a child out of his self-centred bubble, and makes him realize that other people have needs and feelings too – such as the simple need to be acknowledged. *Bonjour* also sets the tone for a child to observe other rules of civility. If he says hello, he's less likely to jump on the sofa. He's been counted as a person – a little person, but a person nonetheless.

47.

Let children 'awaken' and 'discover'

French parents believe it's essential to teach their children about sensory pleasures such as tasting new foods, 'discovering' their bodies through movement (we might call this exercise), or 'awakening' to new sensations like splashing in a pool (this comes long before French children actually learn to swim). Awakening often doesn't require much hard work from parents. It can come from rolling around on a picnic blanket and studying the grass. This probably helps forge some neural pathways. But the real point is to teach children how to enjoy just being in the world.

48.

Leave time for play

A few music or dance classes are fine. But the French believe in giving little children lots of free time. 'When the child plays, he constructs himself,' one of my daughter's Parisian nursery teachers explained. (By design, the nursery gives children lots of unstructured time.) The latest science seems to side with the French. A round-up of neuroscience research couldn't say enough about the benefits of exploratory play: it teaches children persistence, relationship skills and creative problem-solving, improves their attention spans and confidence, and gives them a chance to master activities. Playing isn't just developmentally important – it's also fun.

49.

Let children socialize with people their own size

You know how you crave adult company after being alone with a three-year-old all day? Well, just imagine how that three-year-old feels. French mothers want to spend time with their offspring. But they also think it's crucial that their kids socialize with people who are equally enchanted by fire engines and princess paraphernalia. They want them to learn how to make friends, to wait their turn and to get along in a group. Working parents usually prefer their children to be in a good-quality nursery than alone at home with a nanny. Even stay-at-home mums will often put small children in part-time group care – or spend a lot of time at the local playground.

50.

Back off (and quieten down) at the playground

In France, you don't see parents following their children down the slide or offering a running commentary and encouragement as their offspring play. Nursery teachers say they back off at playtime, to give kids some much-needed freedom. Care-givers believe that once a child can walk securely on his own and climb safely up the slide, their job is to watch from the sidelines as he plays. They don't automatically leap to a child's defence in every playground dispute, but give him a chance to work things out on his own. ('If we intervene all the time, they go a little nuts,' one nursery assistant explained.)

Resist the urge to cross wobbly wooden bridges with your child, or play all his games with him. Just sit on a bench, watch and recharge. That way you'll be a lot more joyful and patient when he does need you.

51.

Extra-curricular activities are for pleasure, not competitive advantage

You're not building a bionic child. Do not take him to violin lessons or read him the twelfth book of the day merely to gain hypothetical IQ points or prepare him for law school. Choose activities that your child enjoys, then let him do them at his own pace. Read the child-development studies if you want to, but don't let them plan your child's day.

52.

It's not just about results

Yes, it's a competitive world. Of course you want to
position your offspring to beat that trilingual rugrat
next door. But childhood is not merely preparation for
the future. The quality of the years you're going to
spend living together matters too. Learn to identify and
enjoy what the French call *moments privilégiés* – little
pockets of joy or calm when you can simply appreciate
being together.

Patience

Wait a Minute

One reason why French family life often feels so calm is that parents emphasize patience. They believe that waiting – and related skills, such as coping with frustration and delaying gratification – can be learned and honed.

The French focus on patience partly because they find the alternative intolerable. They've seen households in which adults are never able to finish a phone call or a cup of coffee, and where kids collapse in hysteria each time they're denied a chocolate bar. They don't want to live that way, or think it's inevitable that they should. And they don't think that living that way would make their children happy either.

53.

Give your child lots of practice at waiting

The secret to patience isn't expecting a child to be a stoic who just freezes and silently waits for you to pay attention to him. Researchers have found that kids become good at waiting when they learn how to distract themselves – by inventing a little song, perhaps, or burping at themselves in the mirror. This makes the waiting bearable.

French parents have discovered this too. They know that they don't even have to teach their children how to distract themselves. If they simply say 'wait' a lot and make a child practise waiting on a daily basis, she'll soon work out how to distract herself. But if they drop everything the instant she complains that she's bored, or if they finish their phone conversation when she interrupts, their child isn't going to become good at waiting. She's going to become good at whining.

54.

Slow down your response times

Embrace a French pace of life. Remember the Pause – it applies to toddlers as well as babies. When you're busy scrambling eggs and your daughter asks you to inspect her tower of toilet-paper rolls, explain nicely that you'll be there in a few minutes, when you've finished. At dinner, don't leap up to grab a napkin the moment she demands it (or better still, put the napkins on a low shelf so she can get one herself). When you're busy, politely point out what you're doing, and ask her to take it in.

This doesn't just make life calmer. It's also what the French call an 'obligatory passage' in which the child learns that she's not the centre of the universe. Parents believe that a child who doesn't realize this – and who feels she's entitled to anything she wants – won't see any reason to grow up.

The French have reasonable expectations. They wouldn't ask a little child to sit through Shakespeare (or Molière). They just want her to be able to wait a few minutes. Slowing things down even this little bit will make her better at coping with boredom, and take the panicky edge off things. Patience is a muscle. The more a child plays on her own, the better she will get at it.

55.

Expect children to control themselves

Play to the top of a child's intelligence. Make it clear that you expect her not to grab things, and to be able to put all her Lego back in its box herself. Get down on the floor and gently tell a toddler who's pulling books off the shelf that she should stop, and show her how to put them back. When a young child tosses grapes on the floor, show her how to keep them on her plate. Do this patiently and face-to-face. A child needs to learn the limits, but she also needs love. 'It takes both love and frustration for the child to construct himself,' one expert explains. If you give the child just love without limits, she'll soon become a little tyrant (the French call this an 'enfant roi' – a child king).

56.

Don't let your child interrupt

When a child interrupts, French parents believe that
you should calmly say something along the lines of
'Excuse me, sweetheart, I'm in the middle of speaking to
someone. Please wait and I'll be with you in a moment.'
Then make good on that promise. Continue the
conversation, then turn back to the child and give her
your attention. Make her wait her turn to speak in
conversations, too, and teach her at least to say 'excuse
me' if it's urgent. ('Urgent' in our house usually means
that the dragon's second head – the less important head,
I always say – has fallen off again.)

Remember that you're not just trying to enjoy the
simple pleasure of finishing your phone call. You're also
teaching your child to respect others and to be aware of
what's happening around her. One French woman I
know says that when her son interrupts, she makes
him stop and look at the person she's speaking to, so
that he fully registers what's going on. 'It's a way of
living together,' she explains. All this practice won't
prevent your child from ever interrupting you again.
But she'll gradually get more in touch with the rhythm
of the room.

57.

It's mutual: don't interrupt your child

Everyone in the household has a right to be absorbed in something, without being interrupted. Whenever your child is happily engaged in an activity, try to avoid charging over with a question or a change of plans. When everyone isn't constantly bursting in on each other, the whole pace of family life slows down a notch.

58.

Observe the French food rules

French food rituals offer a daily exercise in how to delay gratification. Children eat most meals in courses, rather than all at once. They taste all foods, even the ones they don't like – a form of coping with frustration. Even if they're hungry, they wait to eat at mealtimes. If they are given some chocolate in the morning, they typically won't be allowed to eat it until the afternoon *goûter*. With practice, all of this gets much easier; eventually it becomes natural and not arduous at all.

59.

Let them eat cake

Baking is a regular weekend activity for many French families, starting practically from the time when children can sit alone in a chair. Measuring ingredients and following a recipe are excellent lessons in patience. And once the cake is made, families usually wait until *goûter* to eat it. Everybody – parents included – aims to eat reasonable portions (the adults are trying to model restraint for their kids).

60.

Treat coping with frustration as a crucial life skill

French parents don't worry that they'll damage a child by frustrating her. *Au contraire*, they think a child can't be happy if she needs to have things instantly and if she's constantly subject to her own whims. They believe that children derive pride and pleasure from being able to choose how they respond to challenges.

Teaching kids to handle frustration from an early age will also make them more resilient. Young children who are good at delaying gratification are more likely to grow into teenagers who can handle setbacks, and who are good at concentrating and reasoning. Consider it a French paradox: trying to keep young children happy all the time will make them less happy later on.

61.

Cope calmly with tantrums

French parents are just as flummoxed and distressed by tantrums as the rest of us. They don't have a magic recipe to make the crying stop. But what they generally agree on is that you shouldn't concede to an unreasonable demand. ('Above all, don't give in,' one father tells me.) Tantrums don't change the rules.

This doesn't mean that you should be cold. French parents say that children are understandably angry when they can't have or do what they want. Parents try to show sympathy ('Who wouldn't want to have a cookie just before lunch?') and let their children express their discontent. Some say they ask the child what she thinks a good solution would be, given the constraints. If the child can calm down enough to talk, she'll often have some reasonable ideas – like having the same cookie as an afternoon snack.

Sometimes, giving an upset child more autonomy helps. Let her help you prepare dinner, or serve herself. Backing off and letting her do more can change the mood and calm her down. Timing matters, too. Be in touch with her rhythms. Don't expect an overtired child to go grocery shopping or out to dinner.

When a tantrum happens at home and continues for too long, parents typically send the child to her room, and tell her to come out when she's calm again. 'If it's too loud I say, "Go and yell in your room." But I understand that it makes her very angry,' the mother of a five-year-old explains. 'She usually goes into her room and yells, then she comes back out and does what I asked,' this mother claims. If a child manages to come out calmly, parents respond positively and then everyone moves on.

In short, be calm and sympathetic, without giving in.

62.

Teaching patience requires patience

Your child won't become an expert delayer in a day. Learning to wait is part of what the French call her *éducation* – an ongoing process of teaching her skills and values. Be consistent. Whenever you start to waver, consider the alternative.

The Cadre

Free to Be Vous and Moi

When a mother hovers over her child too much in France, someone else is apt to say, 'Just let him live his life!' This is one of the battle cries of French parenting. The French do a lot for their children, but they don't try to clear all obstacles from their paths. Instead, they strive to treat children as independent beings who are able to cope with challenges on their own.

This independence develops at a reasonable pace. Little French children don't drive cars or operate heavy machinery. Parents supervise them closely and judge when their child is ready to take the next step. They believe that when you treat kids as being capable and trustworthy, they will respond by taking on more responsibility for their own actions and by behaving well. And giving kids a bit of space can actually bring you closer.

63.

Give children meaningful chores

Don't underestimate what children can do, with some guidance. It's quite normal for French three- and four-year-olds to have their own chores – to help load the dishwasher after dinner, for instance. (Mothers I know report no more than a few broken plates.) A friend of mine's six-year-old says her favourite activity is taking out the rubbish all by herself. She also proudly describes the time when her mum stayed outside the corner shop and let her go inside alone to buy some lemons.

These small tasks are very meaningful for children, especially if they're performed on a regular basis. When children play an active role in the household, they become more self-reliant and learn that adults are not just there to serve them. Kids also find these activities fun. Obviously, the thrill won't last for ever. But the idea that their contribution to the family matters probably will.

64.

Build your child a cadre

The *cadre* (meaning 'frame' or 'framework') is the closest that most French parents get to having a parenting philosophy. They strive to be very strict about a few key rules and to be consistent about these – that's the *cadre*. But within this framework, they aim to give their children as much freedom as they can handle.

Parents decide which rules are important. Parisians I've met often choose politeness and respect for others, how much screen time their kids are allowed, and what they should eat.

You can apply the *cadre*'s cocktail of strictness and freedom to lots of different situations. Some that I've heard from French parents are:

- At bedtime you have to stay in your room, but inside your room you can do whatever you want.
- You can only watch two hours of television this weekend, but you can choose when to use these two hours and what to watch.
- You have to taste a bit of everything at each meal, but you don't have to eat it all.
- When we go out, I can veto your outfit if it's

inappropriate, but at home you can wear what you want.

- You can't eat sweets whenever you want to, but you can at the *goûter*.
- I won't buy you non-necessities on demand, but you can save up and buy them with your own pocket money. (French children usually start getting monthly pocket money at about the age of seven.)

65.

Everybody needs a swear word

There's a special 'swear word' that French pre-schoolers use: *caca boudin*. This literally translates as 'poop sausage', but it's an all-purpose (and relatively innocent) phrase that can mean 'you wish', 'bollocks' or 'whatever'. No one teaches their child to say *caca boudin*. Kids just pick it up from each other. Their parents might cringe a bit when they hear the phrase, but they tend not to ban it. Instead, they teach their children to wield it appropriately. Some tell them they can only say it in the bathroom, or when they're alone with their friends. They can't say it to teachers, or at dinner. But parents recognize that kids are subject to lots of rules. Sometimes they just need to say *caca boudin*.

66.

Your child can benefit from time away from you

French five-year-olds go on residential school trips without their parents, just their teachers. During school holidays, they'll often spend a week or two on their own with their grandparents. If you can get a grandparent or trusted friend or relative on board, arrange for your child to spend some time away from you. To help these separations go smoothly, give your surrogate just a few basic instructions (don't worry about her doing things differently from you) and try to project cheerful confidence when you're saying goodbye. Start out with an overnight stay, and then move up to a long weekend. 'If everything goes well, he'll come back smarter,' a child psychiatrist explains, referring to children aged three to five. 'You'll find him changed, he will have learned to behave like a big boy. He'll gain in independence.' I won't even start on the benefits to his parents.

67.

Don't be the referee

French parents try to avoid becoming the arbiters of all disputes – whether between siblings, playmates, or new acquaintances at the playground. They try to empower their children with the authority and knowhow to work things out on their own. One father says that when his five-year-old twins argue, he asks them to suggest a solution themselves. (They usually think of something, he says.)

French experts say that sibling rivalry is inevitable, and that the arrival of a new baby is a genuine shock for an older child. In this case, 'you must console him, help him express himself, reassure him, tell him that you understand his anxiety, his sorrow, his jealousy, show him that it's normal for him to have these feelings,' a parenting book says.

68.

Keep the risks in perspective

French parents know about choking hazards, allergies and paedophiles. They take reasonable precautions. But they try not to obsess over the less likely scenarios. Instead, they believe that parents should speak to their children about dangers and how to protect themselves. One expert suggests explaining to a child as young as one that cars are dangerous, so he should never cross the street without an adult.

There is an important difference between shielding a child from danger and cutting him off from the world. Remember that children gain confidence from overcoming difficulties and relying on their own resources. As one French writer warns, 'To grow up without risk is to risk not growing up.'

69.

Don't raise a praise addict

A French mother tells me that instead of saying 'bravo' whenever her five-year-old does something well, she sometimes prefers to ask, 'Are you proud of yourself?' The French believe children don't build self-esteem by being relentlessly assured by their parents that they are doing a good job; they build it by doing new things on their own, and knowing they are doing them well. Praising a child too much can actually be damaging. He'll become so eager to maintain your high opinion of him that he won't want to risk trying something new. Or he'll do things merely to get the brief high that comes from hearing 'bravo', but will lose motivation when you're not around to say it. Of course you should be encouraging – you don't want to under-praise. Just don't overdo it.

70.

Encourage children to speak well

Once a child can speak fluently, French parents and teachers don't automatically coo at everything he says. When he's wildly off topic, they say so and steer him back. At the dinner table, his parents will pay more attention to him when he expresses himself well and says interesting things. This is meant to arm the child with good social skills. (He might get away with prattling on at his grandmother's house, but it will be less charming later when he goes on dates.)

71.

Watch for the 'déclic'

The *déclic* is a eureka moment when a child figures out how to do something important on his own. Something clicks. For young children, it can be the period when they become potty trained, or work out how to make friends. For teenagers, it can be the moment when they stop working to satisfy their parents and start working because they want to succeed for themselves. It's interpreted as a welcome sign of maturity and autonomy. French parents often wait and hope for the *déclic*. Non-French parents do too. It's helpful to have a name for it.

72.

Allow your child to keep a 'jardin secret'

The French believe that everyone is entitled to a
'secret garden' – a private realm. It's part of being an
independent person. Even very involved parents accept
that their children need privacy – particularly as they
grow older – and will have some secrets. They don't
expect to know every detail of their children's lives.
They do expect to know that, generally, everything
is OK.

73.

Respect your child, and he'll respect you

Autonomy is a fundamental need for your child. (Françoise Dolto said that by the age of six, a child should be able to do everything at home that concerns him.) By granting him autonomy, you show that you trust and respect him. You're appealing to his higher self. Give him this, and he's more likely to respect what you need, too. Ideally, as the French say, everyone in the family should get to live his life.

Motherhood

Cherchez la Femme

French mothers strive for a very particular kind of balance in their lives. It's not a keeping-plates-in-the-air kind of balance. It's more like a balanced meal. Just as you wouldn't want to eat only dessert, the French aim is that no one part of your life – being a wife, a worker or a mother – should eclipse the other parts. Even the most devoted maman *is also supposed to devote energy and passion to other things. If she doesn't, everyone suffers, including her children. Not all French mums manage to achieve and maintain just the right* équilibre. *But they at least try to keep it in mind.*

74.

Guilt is a trap

Let's face it: guilt can feel good. It's like a tax you pay for being away from your child. It buys you some free time. As long as you feel guilty about leaving her, you can finally go to yoga class. (Sociologists call this leisure time spent worrying 'contaminated time'.)

French mothers understand the temptation to feel guilty, but they think it's a shame to spoil their precious free time. Instead of embracing guilt, they try to push it away. When they meet up for drinks, they remind each other that 'the perfect mother doesn't exist' and take pride in being able to detach from their children and relax. 'When I'm there I give them 100 per cent, but when I'm off, I'm off,' a mother of three explains.

75.

Show your children that you have a life apart from them

For French mothers, it's not enough to have their own pleasures and interests. They also want their kids to know about these things. They believe it's a burden for a child to feel that she's the sole source of her mother's happiness and satisfaction. (A single mother I know in Paris told me she was going back to work partly for her daughter's sake.)

French women want other adults to see that they have non-mum lives too. Even if they've spent the day folding tiny socks, they try not to talk to others at length about their children's toilet habits. They know that if you act (and dress) as if you have a fascinating inner life, you may soon find that you actually do – and that you feel more balanced as a result.

There are also pragmatic reasons for having a life of your own. Some French women drop out of the work force when they have children, but many go back to their jobs. (State-subsidized crèches and universal nursery education from the age of three certainly make this easier in France than in the UK or USA.) Even women in happy marriages calculate that not earning their own money would leave them financially vulnerable, in case of divorce. And they worry that, *sans* pay cheque, they'll lose status and decision-making power at home, and become less interesting to people outside of it.

76.

Birthday parties are for children

In Paris, from about the age of three, birthday parties and play dates are usually drop-offs. French mothers don't feel they must supervise another adult supervising their child, or stick around to reassure the child herself. They make sure she's in good hands, and then they leave. Often they're invited back for coffee or cocktails at the end. It's a practical way of coping with the fact that all parents are extremely busy, and that – while we're delighted that our kids get along – we're not all actually friends.

77.

Lose the baby weight

For French women, there's no better proof that they haven't morphed from '*femme*' to '*maman*' than getting back their pre-baby figure, or some reasonable facsimile thereof. Parisiennes often aim to do this by three months post-partum.

It helps that they don't allow themselves to gain too much weight while they're pregnant. Many French women also follow a sensible non-deprivation diet as a matter of course, in which during the week they eat smallish portions, consume their main meal at lunchtime, don't snack between meals, and avoid bread, pasta and sugary foods. But at weekends (or on one weekend day) they will eat whatever they want. In other words, they don't vow never to eat lasagne, cakes and croissants again, they just save these for special days. The latest research agrees with their methods. People tend to have more self-control when they don't permanently exclude certain foods from their diet; they just tell themselves that they'll have them later. Studies also recommend closely monitoring your weight (French women call this 'paying attention').

78.

Don't dress like a mum

Unless a French woman is actually holding a child, it's usually very hard to tell if she's a mother. There's no tell-tale look, or type of trousers. They don't sex it up to over-compensate (there's no French equivalent of a 'yummy mummy', because in France there's no reason why any mum wouldn't be considered sexy). But they don't walk around wearing sweatpants and scrunchies either – even if they're heading to the gym. Instead, they seek an elegant middle ground. French mothers don't feel selfish for caring about their appearance. (In the French edition of *Marie Claire*, a mum of three confesses that she's sometimes so busy *she wears unmatched bras and panties*.) They know that looking good improves morale and makes you feel more balanced. It just does.

79.

Don't become a 'taxi mother'

In Paris, it's seen as perfectly reasonable to consider the impact on your own quality of life when making choices for your child. A French woman who spends most of her free time shuttling her kids between extra-curricular activities isn't seen as a devoted mother – she's viewed as a woman who has dramatically lost her balance. Her sacrifice isn't even considered good for her children. They may want to do judo and learn the piano, but they also need to have unstructured time at home. A French psychologist says there's a crucial difference between being responsive and attentive to your child, and becoming a 'vending machine' who's always on.

80.

You're allowed to be happier than your least happy child

Really you are. It doesn't mean that you're a bad person. It means you're a separate person, with your own needs and temperament. See if you can empathize with your child without taking on her emotions. In fact, it's better to respond to an upset child with objectivity and calm. You're modelling the way you'd like her to feel.

Your
Relationship
Adult Time

*French experts say that in the first few months after a
baby is born, his parents should – indeed must – give
themselves over completely to his care. They're in the
fusionelle phase, when it's all about the baby. Some call
this, presidentially, 'the first hundred days'.*

*But some time around the three-month mark, couples
expect to start gradually 'finding their couple' again.
There's no fixed schedule. You're not supposed to
abandon the baby and jump on the next flight to Bali. It's
more of a rebalancing, during which you 'relearn the
contours of intimacy' – both physically and emotionally –
and make space in the family home where just the two of
you can be together.*

81.

Your baby doesn't replace your partner

He's cuddly, he's adorable, and your mother loves him. But your baby shouldn't permanently nudge your partner out of the picture. 'The family is based on the couple. If it exists only through children, it withers,' a French psychologist explains. In some families, the three-month mark is the point when the baby starts sleeping in his own room. Until then he may have been in a Moses basket in his parents' room, or even in their bed. (Long-term co-sleeping is very rare in France, in part because it prevents relations between Mum and Dad from getting back to normal.)

The French famously believe that all healthy people – old people, ugly people, even new parents – should have a sex drive. A leading French parenting magazine says that if your libido hasn't returned by four to six months post-partum, you should seek professional help.

82.

Your bedroom is your castle

Guard it carefully. Your child doesn't have the right to barge in whenever he wants. For starters, you need sleep. Explain to him that in the morning you want him to play in his room until it's very light outside (or teach him to read a digital clock, and explain that he can't come in until the first number is an eight – or a seven on school days).

It's also important for him to understand – through tender gestures and closed doors – that there's a part of his parents' lives that doesn't involve him. 'My parents' room was a sacred place, different from the rest of the house,' one French woman recalls. 'You didn't just walk in, you had to have a good reason. Between them there was an obvious pleasure that implied something unknown for us, the children.' If your child believes he already has it all – that there's no mysterious adult world to aspire to – why should he bother to grow up?

83.

Beware of 'le baby-clash'

The French swoon for babies, but they're also clear-eyed about how hard little ones can be on a relationship. The parenting press regularly warns about '*le baby-clash*' – the risk of couples separating in the child's first two years, because of the loss of freedom and the shock of suddenly having to function as parents. Experts don't have a magic solution for this problem, but say it's helpful to see it coming. ('It's not us, honey, it's *le baby-clash*!') They urge couples to reignite intimacy, discuss problems with each other, and clearly divvy up baby duties.

84.

Pretend to agree

No matter how misguided your partner's proclamations about the household rules are, never contradict him in front of the children. Wait and speak to him in private. He should do the same for you. That way, you'll build complicity between you. And since the rules aren't up for discussion, they'll have more force. You'll both seem more authoritative to your kids, and they'll also be reassured by the impression that there's something solid and united at the family's core.

85.

Don't aim for absolute equality

Expecting your partner to do half the housework and childcare can be a recipe for resentment and conflict. (This explains why, when British and American women get together, it's only a matter of minutes before they start ranting about their husbands.) Try to temper your modern feminist beliefs with some old-fashioned French pragmatism. French women would love their partners to do more, but many settle for a division of labour that isn't fifty–fifty, but that more or less works. They try to weigh the ideal of complete equality against the advantages of having a husband who's calm and de-stressed after his Saturday-morning rugby match. And they've discovered that there's less conflict when everyone has his or her own tasks to perform at home – even if the actual hours each partner puts in aren't equal. Paradoxically, if you're less angry, you might want to have more sex, and your partner might do more around the house as a result.

86.

Fathers are a separate species

Many French women treat their men as adorable but hapless creatures who are genetically incapable of keeping track of the kids' inoculation schedules and remembering to buy the cheese. Of course they come home with the wrong cereals, and with strawberries that look as if they've been beaten with a mallet. They're men – they just can't help it! (One French woman told me, with mock exasperation, that her husband makes only his side of the bed.)

French mums say they try not to throw a tantrum when they come home from a business trip to find their house besieged by dirty laundry. It's possible that the poor fellow was, actually, doing his best.

87.

Praise mum for her mastery of the mundane

Centuries of expert courtship have taught French men that you cannot over-praise a woman. So French fathers sometimes try to compensate for their shortcomings at home by marvelling at the dull and time-consuming tasks their wives perform, and by confessing that such multi-tasking is beyond them. (When said gallantly, this sounds less patronizing than you'd expect.) If their partner doesn't have a paying job, French men are wise enough never to ask, 'What did you do all day?'

88.

Maintain some mystery in your marriage

You are not a publicly traded company. You don't owe your shareholder – er, spouse – total transparency. I'm not suggesting you should have an affair or commit crimes in secret (contrary to British popular belief, while French presidents tend not to be terribly faithful, ordinary French citizens rarely cheat on their partners). But do keep a bit of mystery in your marriage, *à la française*. Let there be innuendo, knowing glances, and things left unsaid. Flirt with others, too, if you want to. Realize that you can feel energized by these interactions without their leading inexorably to adultery and death.

89.

Evenings should be adult time

After the stories, songs and cuddles, French parents are firm about bedtime. They believe that having some child-free time in the evenings is not an occasional privilege, it's a fundamental human right. Ditto spending the occasional evening out or escaping for a restorative long weekend *à deux*. The French don't have an equivalent of the English phrase 'date night'. When they can arrange it, they just go out together – the way our parents used to. They consider a solid and loving marriage to be essential to the happy functioning of the whole family. If you explain this to your kids, they will accept it too.

90.

No teepees in the living room

The French know that it's hard to relax and enjoy adult time when you're staring at a miniature plastic kitchen. They typically don't let children's toys and games reside permanently in the living room. Make a family ritual of putting them back in the kids' rooms before bedtime. Keep a (non-Technicolor) box in the living room where you can stash stray stuffed animals and doll extremities. Don't let baby-proofing be your dominant interior-design motif.

Authority

Just Say 'Non'

Another battle cry of French parenting is 'C'est moi qui décide' ('It's me who decides'). You can hear parents say – and occasionally shout – this phrase, to remind their children and themselves who's in charge, and to shift the balance of power back in their favour. Just uttering the words is fortifying. (Try saying them. You'll feel your back stiffen.)

To be the decider, you don't have to be an ogre. French parents don't want to turn their children into obedient robots. But they still agree with Jean-Jacques Rousseau's contention, made 250 years ago, that perpetual negotiations are bad for children. 'The worst education is to leave him floating between his will and yours, and to dispute endlessly between you and him as to which of the two will be the master.'

91.

Say 'no' with conviction

The French didn't invent the word 'no', but they're especially good at saying it. They don't worry that refusing a child something will limit his creativity or crush his spirit. They believe that children blossom best within set limits and find it reassuring to know that a grown-up is steering the ship.

The French '*non*' is convincing partly because parents don't say it constantly. They believe that a few strategically administered refusals have a better chance of registering with kids than a blizzard of them.

But the real secret is the unambivalent delivery. Kids can tell when you really mean 'no' and won't back down. You don't have to shout. Just look your child in the eye, kneeling down to his level if you have to, and say it with calm confidence. This takes some practice. When you get it right, you'll feel it. You won't just sound more authoritative to your child – you will actually believe that you are the boss.

92.

Say 'yes' as often as you can

The French believe that another key to having authority over your child is to say 'yes' as often as you can. (One expert points out that 'authority' has the same root as 'authorize'.) It can take some recalibrating to make your default answer become 'yes', but doing so has a calming effect. Your child will feel more respected and more trusted as a result, and she will get to satisfy her desire to do things for herself. Of course, total freedom would be overwhelming. The ideal French scenario is that a child will ask permission to do something, and the parent will grant it.

93.

Explain the reason behind the rule

When you say 'no', you should always explain why. You're not trying to scare your child into obeying you. Rather, you want to create a world that's coherent and predictable to her, and to show that you respect her autonomy and intelligence.

If a situation is dangerous, act first and give your reason afterwards. Be straightforward and matter-of-fact: you don't want your explanation to sound like a negotiation – it's not. Sometimes it helps to remind kids of the rules. One French mother says that each time she walks into the supermarket, she tells her two girls that they're there to buy necessities for the house, not treats like toys or sweets. She says she's been so consistent about applying this that the girls don't even ask for treats any more (though they can choose to buy them with their pocket money).

When speaking to kids, French parents will often talk in terms of rights, for example: 'You don't have the right to bite Pierre.' This suggests that there's a coherent system of rules, and that the child *does* have the right to do other things.

94.

Sometimes your child will hate you

French psychologists say that children's desires are practically limitless. Your job, as a parent, is to stop this chain of wanting by sometimes saying 'no'. The child will probably get angry when you do this. She might even temporarily hate you. This isn't a sign that you're a terrible parent. 'If the parent isn't there to stop him, then he's the one who's going to have to stop himself or not stop himself, and that's much more anxiety-provoking,' one psychologist explains. In other words, if you need your child to like you all the time, you simply cannot do your job. Be strong, and your child will, as the French say, 'find her place'.

95.

De-dramatize

This word crops up a lot in France, when it comes to dealing with upset or cranky children of all ages. The idea is that you should defuse moments of conflict by responding calmly, or by lightening the mood with a joke.

Avoid castigating your child in front of others. One French mother told me she suspected that her teenage daughter had been smoking cigarettes during a sleepover, but she waited until the friend left the next morning before confronting her daughter. 'If you make a scene in front of her friends, she will stop talking to you,' she explained.

With older children, aim to exercise your authority without losing your connection with them. If you're so angry that you need time to cool off, say so. 'I don't think the world of children is so far from the world of adults. They're capable of understanding everything,' this French mum said.

96.

You're not disciplining, you're educating

The next time your child speaks with a mouth full of pasta, remember that you're teaching her table manners gradually, in the same way that you would teach her maths. In other words, the learning doesn't happen all at once. As the French say, you're giving her an '*éducation*', which starts when children are very young. Unlike discipline, *éducation* (which has nothing to do with school) is something that French parents imagine themselves to be doing all the time. Reminding yourself that you're 'educating' will help you feel less angry and disrespected when the occasional slice of cucumber lands on your lap.

Don't jump on your child for every offence. The French call a small act of naughtiness a *bêtise*. Using this word helps keep the crime in perspective too. When your child jumps on the sofa or swipes a piece of bread off the counter before dinner, she's just done a *bêtise*. All kids do them sometimes. Save your punishments for the felonies. It will help her learn what's important.

97.

Make 'the big eyes'

In France, one suitable response to a *bêtise* is to give a child 'the big eyes'. It's a disapproving, owl-like stare that serves as a warning. It means that you saw what your child did, and she should watch her step. 'The important thing is that he knows he's breaking a rule,' one mother tells me. This can be a surprisingly effective deterrent.

98.

Give children time to comply

You're running a family, not a military battalion. Don't expect your child to jump to attention as soon as you issue an order. Explain what you'd like her to do, then watch and wait for her to comply. Obviously you're applying pressure, but you also want to give her autonomy over how and at what speed she obeys. It's more likely to be an effective, long-term lesson if she feels as if she has some say in the matter.

99.

Punish rarely, but make it count

To be *puni* in a French family is a big deal. It's not something that happens every night at dinner. French childcare experts say a punishment should be administered immediately and matter-of-factly, without malice. Parents typically send a young naughty child to her room to 'marinate' or think on it, and tell her to come out when she's calm again and ready to talk. For older children, the punishment is often a few days without TV, computers or video games, or taking away the child's phone for a week.

Parents say they're careful to warn children before punishing them, and to make sure they follow through on their threats. They also try to be fair at the other end – for instance, by returning the phone promptly on the promised day. After a conflict, they say it's the parent's role to re-establish the connection between the two of them again, for example by suggesting that they play a favourite game together. They try to teach children that after the storm comes calm.

100.

Sometimes there's nothing you can do

There are times when nothing will console your child, or make her listen to you. That's OK. Accept her reaction, and wait it out. Remember, you're on a long-term mission to educate. You don't have to win every battle.

Favourite Recipes from the Parisian Crèche

These dishes are eaten by children, aged three and under, who attend Paris's public nurseries. They're cooked from scratch by in-house chefs, then served as part of four-course meals composed of a starter, a main course and side dish, a cheese course, and then a fruit dessert (children under twelve months only get two courses). A crèche nutritionist has adapted the quantities for family dining: each recipe serves two adults and two children.

Appetizers and Side Dishes

Carottes râpées à l'orange
(grated carrots with orange)

   3 carrots
   2 tbsp vegetable oil
   Juice of 1 orange
   ⅛ clove crushed garlic (or a pinch of dried garlic)
   Pinch of salt

Wash, peel and grate the carrots.

Mix the oil, juice, garlic and salt in a small bowl.

Pour this mixture over the grated carrots and toss.

(This dish can be prepared just before serving. It's also delicious after marinating overnight.)

Velouté d'artichaut à la crème
(creamy artichoke soup)

> 1 large potato
> 2 shallots, finely chopped
> 2 tbsp olive oil
> 6 tinned artichoke bottoms, diced
> 600ml water
> Salt
> 2 tbsp crème fraîche (or sour cream)
> Herbs (parsley, basil or coriander, chopped)

Wash and peel the potato. Cut it into large pieces.

In a large pan or casserole dish, sauté the shallots in a little olive oil until soft.

Add the potato and artichoke pieces. Sauté them for 2 to 3 minutes.

Cover the vegetables with water, add a bit of salt and cook for about 40 minutes. Add the crème fraîche and mix.

Keep the soup warm until you're ready to eat it. Add a pinch of chopped herbs before serving.

Brocoli braisé
(braised broccoli)

> 450g broccoli, fresh or frozen
> Salt
> 15g unsalted butter

Steam fresh broccoli for 4 to 5 minutes or submerge it in boiling water for 5 to 6 minutes. (If frozen, steam for 8 to 10 minutes or boil for 10 to 12 minutes.) The broccoli should remain firm, not mushy. Saving some of the cooking water, drain the broccoli well. Add a pinch of salt.

Melt the butter in a pan. Sauté the broccoli in the butter over a medium heat until it's tender. If the broccoli is still too firm, add a bit of the cooking water and let it cook for another minute or so.

Main Courses

Saumon à la créole
(salmon creole)

This dish has become a staple in Parisian crèches, thanks to the many in-house chefs who hail from the French Caribbean.

> 1 medium onion, chopped
> 2 tbsp sunflower or olive oil
> 250ml chopped skinless tomatoes, tinned or fresh
> ½ tsp thyme, chopped
> 1 bay leaf
> ½ tsp parsley, chopped
> Salt and pepper
> 3 or 4 medium-sized salmon fillets, fresh or frozen
> Juice of 1 lemon

Preheat the oven to 200°C.

In a large pan, sauté the onion in the oil.

Add the tomatoes, thyme, bay leaf, parsley, salt and pepper. Cover and simmer for 15 minutes.

Place the salmon fillets in an ovenproof dish. Squeeze the lemon juice over the salmon, then spoon on the tomato mixture.

Cover the dish with some foil and bake in the oven until cooked thoroughly: about 20 minutes, or 40 minutes if the salmon is frozen. Before serving, remove the bay leaf and any bones, and add a pinch of parsley or chives to each plate. Serve with rice and some vegetables (braised broccoli is recommended).

Flan de courgettes
(courgette flan)

  2 shallots, finely chopped
  2 tbsp olive oil
  3 medium-sized courgettes
  4 eggs
  200ml crème fraîche (or sour cream)
  ¼ tsp salt
  ¼ tsp ground nutmeg
  60g grated cheese (Gruyère or similar)

Preheat oven to 180°C.

Wash and peel the courgettes. Cook them whole, either by steaming them for 9 minutes or by submerging them in boiling water for 15 minutes. Drain them well and cut them into thin round slices.

Sauté the shallots in the olive oil.

In a bowl, mix the eggs, crème fraîche, salt and nutmeg. Add the shallots. Don't overmix.

Line an ovenproof dish with greaseproof paper (if you have some). Arrange a layer of courgettes in the bottom of the dish and cover them completely with some of the egg mixture. Add another layer of courgettes and cover with more egg mixture. Keep doing this until you've used up all the ingredients.

Sprinkle the cheese over the top and bake for 30 to 40 minutes.

Optional (but highly recommended): top each serving of flan with a bit of warm tomato coulis (see below).

Tomato coulis

4 large ripe tomatoes (or 1 tin chopped tomatoes)
3 tbsp olive oil
1 clove garlic, peeled and left whole
½ tsp thyme, chopped
½ tsp parsley, chopped
1 bay leaf
½ tbsp sugar
Salt and pepper to taste

If you're using fresh tomatoes, cut the skin at their base and plunge them into boiling water for 30 seconds so you can easily remove the skin. Peel, seed and dice them.

Heat the oil in a saucepan. Add the garlic, thyme, parsley, bay

leaf, tomatoes, sugar, salt and pepper. Cover and simmer for 20
to 25 minutes on low heat.

Remove the garlic clove and bay leaf before serving.

Potage complet lentilles
(lentil soup meal-in-one)

> 300g green lentils
> 2 medium potatoes, peeled and chopped into
>   medium-sized pieces
> 1.2 litres cold water
> 1 clove garlic, chopped
> Black pepper
> ½ tsp cumin
> 2 shallots, chopped
> Salt
> 2 medium carrots, peeled and chopped
> 1 boneless chicken breast, finely diced
> Olive oil
> ¼ cup crème fraîche (or sour cream)
> Parsley, chopped

In a large saucepan, sauté the shallots in some olive oil, add
the lentils and potatoes, and cover with the cold water. Add
the garlic, black pepper, cumin and carrots.

Bring to the boil and simmer, covered, over a medium heat for

45 minutes or until the potatoes and lentils are soft. Add more water if needed. Season with salt. Stir the crème fraîche into the lentils (you can mix in less cream if you want, or just add a dollop to each bowl before serving).

While the lentils are cooking, brown the chicken in a little olive oil in a frying pan.

Pour the soup into bowls, then add some chicken and a pinch of parsley to each.

Desserts

Purée de poire et banane
(pear and banana purée)

> 2 large pears (or 3 small ones)
> 2 bananas
> Juice of ½ lemon
> 60ml water

Wash and peel the pears and bananas. Cut them into pieces.

In a medium-sized saucepan, cook all the ingredients for 15 to 20 minutes over low heat, stirring occasionally.

Take the mixture off the heat and allow it to cool for a few minutes.

When it's no longer steaming, pour it into small cups. Cover and refrigerate them until mealtime.

Pomme au four à la cannelle
(baked apple with cinnamon)

> 4 apples (any cooking apples, or Granny Smith or
>   Golden Delicious)
> 20g unsalted butter
> 4 tsp sugar
> Cinnamon

Preheat the oven to 180ºC.

Wash and partly core the whole apples, leaving a bit of core at
the bottom if you can.

Put a knob of butter and then a teaspoon of sugar in the
centre of each apple. Sprinkle some cinnamon over the top.

Put a few millimetres of water in a baking dish (to keep the
apples from sticking), then place the apples in the dish.

Cook for 20 to 30 minutes, until the apples are soft.

Remove the apples from the water. Serve them warm or cold.

Gâteau au chocolat
(chocolate cake)

    Butter and flour to grease the tin
    160g dark cooking chocolate
    100g unsalted butter
    80g sugar
    40g flour
    3 large eggs (or 4 small ones), separated
    Salt
    Crème fraiche (to serve)

Preheat the oven to 180°C. Grease and flour a 16cm cake tin.

Slowly melt the chocolate and butter in a microwave, or in a saucepan over very low heat.

Remove the chocolate mixture from the heat. While mixing with a wooden spoon, slowly sprinkle in the sugar, then the flour. Add the egg yolks one by one, and stir.

In a bowl, beat the egg whites with a pinch of salt until they form stiff peaks. Gently fold them into the chocolate mixture. Do not overmix.

Immediately pour the mixture into the cake tin and bake for 30 minutes.

Let the cake cool. Serve with a dollop of crème fraîche.

Sample Weekly Lunch Menu from the Parisian Crèche

Monday

18 months to 3 years

Tomato salad with lemon and herbs
~
Fillet of hake with lemon-butter sauce
Spinach with béchamel sauce
~
Mimolette cheese (a hard, orange, cow's milk cheese)
~
Apple and strawberry purée

12 to 18 months

Tomato salad with lemon and herbs
~
Chopped fillet of hake with lemon sauce
Spinach purée
~
Coulommier cheese (a soft cow's milk cheese
that resembles Brie)
~
Apple and strawberry purée

Under 12 months

Mashed fillet of hake with lemon sauce
~
Spinach purée
~
Apple and strawberry purée

Tuesday

18 months to 3 years

Cream of leek soup

~

Chopped turkey with basil sauce

Ratatouille with rice

~

Chanteneige cheese (a spreadable white cheese)

~

Fresh kiwi

12 to 18 months

Cream of leek soup

~

Chopped turkey with basil sauce

Puréed courgette

~

Chanteneige cheese

~

Fresh kiwi

Under 12 months

Mashed turkey with basil sauce

~

Puréed courgette

~

Pear and apple purée

Wednesday

18 months to 3 years

Grated red cabbage with *fromage blanc* (soft white cheese)
~
Slow-cooked lamb with carrots and tomatoes
Couscous
~
White Tomme cheese (a firm cow's milk cheese)
~
Banana and rhubarb compote

12 to 18 months

Grated red cabbage with *fromage blanc*
~
Chopped slow-cooked lamb with carrots and tomatoes
Puréed mushrooms
~
White Tomme cheese
~
Banana and rhubarb compote

Under 12 months

Finely chopped slow-cooked lamb with carrot and tomatoes
~
Puréed mushrooms
~
Banana and rhubarb compote

Thursday

18 months to 3 years

Wheat, tomato and green pepper salad

~

Gratin of endives and ham

~

Roquefort cheese

~

Fresh clementine

12 to 18 months

Macedonian salad (green beans, carrots, celery and flageolet beans in a lemon sauce)

~

Chopped ham

Fresh endive purée

~

Roquefort cheese

~

Fresh clementine

Under 12 months

Finely chopped ham

~

Fresh endive purée

~

Clementine and apple purée

Friday

18 months to 3 years

Grated carrot salad

~

Fillet of salmon in lemon-dill sauce
Pasta twists with butter

~

Goat's cheese

~

Baked apples

12 to 18 months

Finely grated carrot salad

~

Chopped fillet of salmon in lemon-dill sauce
Broccoli purée

~

Goat's cheese

~

Baked apples

Under 12 months

Mashed fillet of salmon in lemon-dill sauce

~

Broccoli purée

~

Apple purée

Bibliography

Baumeister, Roy F. and John Tierney, *Willpower:
Rediscovering the Greatest Human Strength*, New York:
Penguin Press, 2011.

Bloom, Paul, 'Moral Life of Babies', *New York Times
Magazine*, 3 May 2010.
http://www.nytimes.com/2010/05/09/magazine/
09babiest.html?pagewanted=all

Bronson, Po and Ashley Merryman, *NurtureShock:
New Thinking About Children*, New York: Twelve,
2009.

Brunet, Christine and Nadia Benlakhel, *C'est pas bientôt
fini ce caprice? Les calmer sans s'énerver*, Paris: Albin
Michel, 2005.

Carroll, Raymonde, *Cultural Misunderstandings: The French-American Experience*, Chicago: University of Chicago Press, 1990.

Delahaye, Marie-Claude, *Livre de bord de la future maman*, Paris: Marabout, 2007.

De Leersnyder, Hélène, *L'enfant et son sommeil*, Paris: Robert Laffont, 1998.

Doctissimo.fr, 'Enfants tyrans: un peu de bon sens!' Interview with Didier Pleux. http://www.doctissimo.fr/html/psychologie/mag_2003/mag1024/ps_7167_enfants_tyrans_bon_sens_itw.htm

Famili.fr, 'La reprise de la sexualité après bébé'. http://www.famili.fr/,la-reprise-de-la-sexualite-apres-bebe, 438,10193.asp

Famili.fr, 'Devenir parents et rester amants?' http://www.famili.fr/,devenir-parents-et-rester-amants, 599,280849.asp

Dolto, Françoise, *Lorsque l'enfant paraît*, volume 1, Paris: Éditions du Seuil, 1977.

Dolto, Françoise and Danielle Marie Lévy, *Parler juste aux enfants*, Paris: Gallimard, 2002.

Gallais, Marie, 'Impossible de s'occuper seule', *Parents*,
    October 2012, pp. 99–100.

Gravillon, Isabelle *et al.*, 'Nos enfants sont-ils trop protégés?',
    Enfant Magazine, September 2012, pp. 56–7.

Haberfeld, Ingrid, 'Quel est l'impact du stress sur la
    grossesse?', *Parents*, April 2012, pp. 60–61.

Heckman, James J., 'Schools, skills and synapses'.
    http://www.heckmanequation.org/content/resource/
    presenting-heckman-equation

Henry, Dominique, 'Il part sans vous, et c'est bon
    pour lui!', *Famili*, August/September 2012, pp. 104–6.

Kahneman, Daniel and Alan B. Kruege, 'Developments in
    the Measurement of Subjective Well-Being', *Journal of
    Economic Perspectives*, 20(1), 2006, pp. 3–24.

Marcelli, Daniel, *Il est permis d'obéir*, Paris: Albin Michel, 2009.

Marchi, Catherine, '12 conseils pour faire le bonheur de
    votre enfant', *Parents*, August 2010, pp. 52–4.

Mindell, Jodi *et al.*, 'Behavioral treatment of bedtime
    problems and night wakings in young children: AASM
    standards of practice', *Sleep*, 29, 2006, pp. 1263–76.

National Institutes of Health, 'Child care linked to assertive, noncompliant, and aggressive behaviors; vast majority of children within normal range', 16 July 2003.

Ochs, Elinor and Carolina Izquierdo, 'Responsibility in childhood: three developmental trajectories', *Ethos* 37(4), 2009, pp. 391–413.

Ollivier, Debra, *What French Women Know About Love, Sex, and Other Matters of Heart and Mind*, New York: G. P. Putnam's Sons, 2009.

Pernoud, Laurence, *J'élève mon enfant*, Paris: Éditions Horay, 2007.

Pinella, Teresa and Leann L. Birch, 'Help me make it through the night: behavioral entrainment of breast-fed infants' sleep patterns', *Pediatrics* 91(2), 1993, pp. 436–43.

Programme National Nutrition Santé, 'La santé vient en mangeant et en bougeant', 2004.

Renard, Gaëlle, *Au secours! Elle veut des fraises*, Leduc.S Éditions, 2012.

Rossant, Lyonel and Jacqueline Rossant-Lumbroso, *Votre enfant: guide à l'usage des parents*, Paris: Robert Laffont, 2006.

Rousseau, Jean-Jacques, *Émile or On Education*, trans. Allan Bloom, New York: Basic Books, 1979.

Senior, Jennifer, 'All Joy and No Fun', *New York*, 12 July 2010.

Sethi, Anita, Walter Mischel, J. Lawrence Aber, Yuichi Shoda and Monica Larrea Rodriguez, 'The role of strategic attention deployment in development of self-regulation: predicting preschoolers' delay of gratification from mother–toddler interactions', *Developmental Psychology* 36(6), November 2000, pp. 767–77.

Thirion, Marie and Marie-Josèphe Challamel, *Le sommeil, le rêve et l'enfant: de la naissance à l'adolescence*, Paris: Albin Michel, 2002.

Twenge, Jean M., W. Keith Campbell and Craig A. Foster, 'Parenthood and Marital Satisfaction: A Meta-Analytic Review', *Journal of Marriage and Family*, 65(3), August 2003, pp. 574–83.

Winter, Pam, 'Engaging families in the early childhood development story; neuroscience and early childhood development: summary of selected literature and key messages for parenting', Education Services Australia Ltd, 2010.

'Mon enfant à l'école maternelle'.
   http://cache.media.education.gouv.fr/file/Espace_parent
   /35/9/Guide_pratique_des_parents_ecole_maternelle_
   227359.pdf

Author's interview with Sandra Merle, 20 September 2012.

Author's interview with Walter Mischel, 20 July 2010.

Author's interview with Caroline Thompson, 20 April 2010.

Acknowledgements

This book exists thanks to Ann Godoff, Suzanne Gluck, Marianne Velmans and Virginia Smith – who valiantly edited the manuscript while trapped by a hurricane.

Thanks to nutritionist Sandra Merle at the Direction des Familles et de la Petite Enfance in Paris for providing the recipes, and for tolerating my many questions about them. I'm also grateful to Claire Smith, who worked tirelessly to test them (and to baby Kate and others who were made to eat them). My thanks to Adam Kuper and Sapna Gupta for their comments on the manuscript; and to Sarah Hutson, Aislinn Casey and Kate Samano. To my indefatigable illustrator Margaux Motin: thank you for making my legs look twice as long as they actually are.

I'm extremely grateful to readers of *French Children Don't Throw Food*, who wrote to me with questions, comments, stories and encouragement. Your enthusiasm inspired this book. *Merci* to the many French parents who allowed me to ask them questions and observe them in their natural habitat, including Frédérique Souverain, Ingrid Callies, Christophe Delin, Solange Martin, Esther Zajdenweber, Cécile Agon, Christophe Dunoyer, Aurèle Cariès, Benjamin Barda and Véronique Bouruet-Aubertot.

The paradox of writing a parenting book is that you must avoid your own family in order to finish it. My gratitude, always, to Bonnie and Hank. Thank you to Leo, Leila and Joey for their patience (and love). Most of all, thank you to Simon – their father and my husband. *Après toi, le déluge.*

Pamela Druckerman is a freelance journalist on lifestyle issues, married to an English football writer. They live in Paris and have three young children. She is the author of *Lust in Translation* and *French Children Don't Throw Food* (published in America as *Bringing Up Bébé*).